Atomium Bruxelles

The idea that matter is made up of discrete units has emerged since antiquity. The word "atom"
was invented by the ancient Greek philosophers.

Atoms make up the Earth and its inhabitants.

Although the atom is the smallest unit in which matter can be divided, with characteristic properties of a chemical element, it is the basic block of chemistry.

Trips
best
HOLIDAYS

.

The atom,
the symbol of Brussels, is a model
of a unit cell in aniron crystal -
each sphere representing an atom
is made up of 9spheres, 9
interconnected atoms,
whichmakeup the structure of the
molecule.
With a total height of 102 m and a
total mass in 1958 of
2400 tons, this spectacular edifice
symbolizes the vision of a modern
world, peace between nations with
great strides in atomic energy.
The spheres have a diameter of 18
m, that of the tubes is 3.20 m, the
whole construction resting on 3
pillars.

The 9 spheres are connected by
tubes but only 5 of them are open
tothe public,
each with a specific destination:
the shopping area where you
canfind original gifts,
scientific exhibition,
restaurant,
a permanent
exhibition with an archive of
photos and videos for those who
want to
relive the Expo 58 experience, and
the top sphere offers a
magnificent view over Brussels.

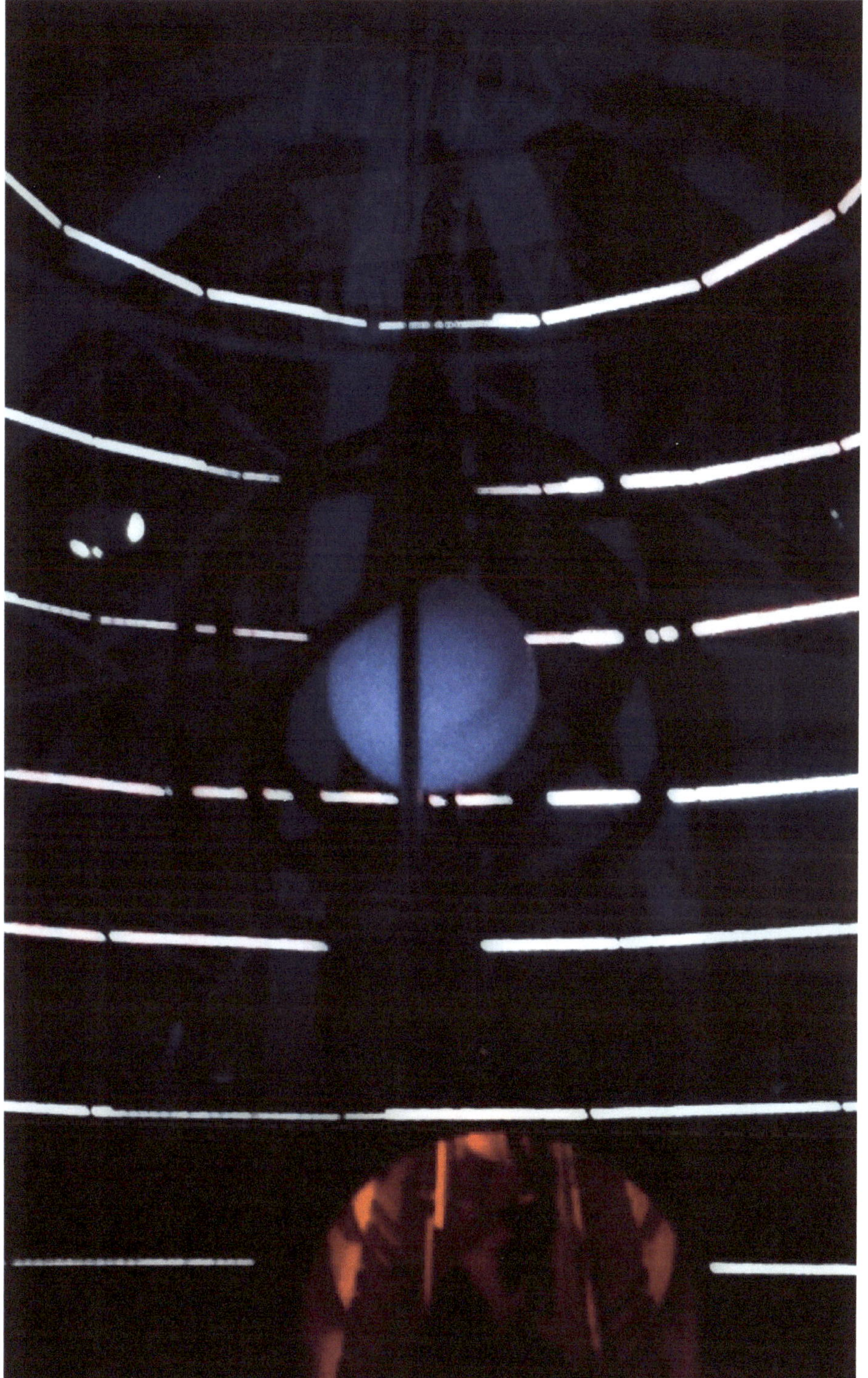

The view offered by the 9 spheres
that are illuminated
by 2970 light bulbs at night is
wonderful.

The central sphere was named after
André Waterkeyn, and the base
sphere after
Henri Storck.
The central and upper spheres are
accessible
only by lift
and the rest by escalators.

But you may be wondering who
André Waterkeyn is...

Well, the Belgian engineer
André Waterkeyn
is the one under whose guidance the
construction of
the symbol began in 1957, being
inaugurated later in 1958 at the
World Fair in Brussels - Expo 58.
International fair where countries
presented special works
attended by 44 countries.
The world fairs were of great
importance to the public,
where they could discover the
evolution of
industrial technology as evidenced by
today's important constructions
and objectives,
such as the Eiffel Tower, the Magic
Fountain in
Montjuic, Barcelona, which
were actually built for
these international exhibitions.

André Waterkeyn made the
model of the future construction
with the help of knitting needles
and tennis balls
- a story told even by
his son Patrick Waterkeyn,
who was a 12-year-old kid at the time.

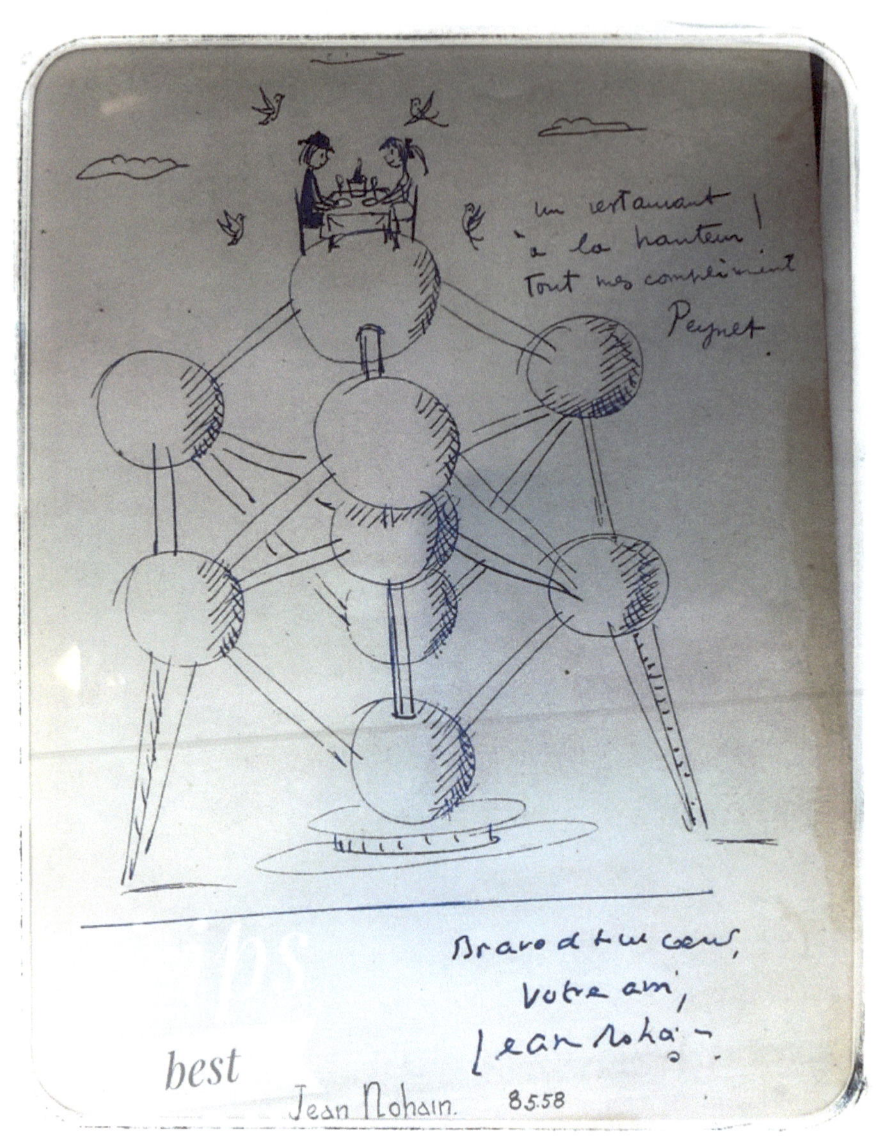

"I remember this model was very solid,
and to prove it,
my father urged us children to climb on it,
the model resisted and no
matter how funny it may seem, this is the
truth."

But this is how it allstarted...

Following the Belgian
Revolution of 1830,
Belgium gained its independence
and every 25th since 1855
Belgium organized
numerous events for celebration.
In 1955 the Belgian government
gave up organizing the event
in order to
have additional funding for the 1958
Exhibition.
However, after Expo 58,
the 11th hosted world fair,
Belgium no longer organized world
fairs.

The international exhibition,
which the Belgians
called the Exposition Universelle et
Internationale de Bruxelles 1958,
was opened with a call for world
peace and social and economic
progress issued by King Baudoin I.

The construction has recorded
over time a series of records
such as:
- 6th place, in1958,
for the highest metal structure
in the world;
-the fastest elevator in the world, in
1958, with a speed of 5 m per
second (18 km / h)
could transport up to 500 people per
hour;
-the fastest stairs in Europe,
in 1958, the 35 m ladder could
carry up
to 3000 people per hour.

Atomium was completely restored in 2006,

A former tour guide, Wim Laernarts,
a former Atomium tour guide,
proudly states:

*"The primary structure
was much better highlighted,
before the spheres
were covered with cardboard and an
insulating material.
Many young
people are delighted with this
construction,
some would even like to
live in it because it inspires
a sense of freedom."*

TRIPS BEST
HOLIDAYS

TRIPS BEST
HOLIDAYS

Atomium is located quite far from the city center in the Larken area, about 10 kmfrom GrandPlace. You can get here by metro - line 6, direction Roi Baudouin Koning - Bowdewijn, to Heyzel station(Heisel),
tram 7 or buses 84,88.

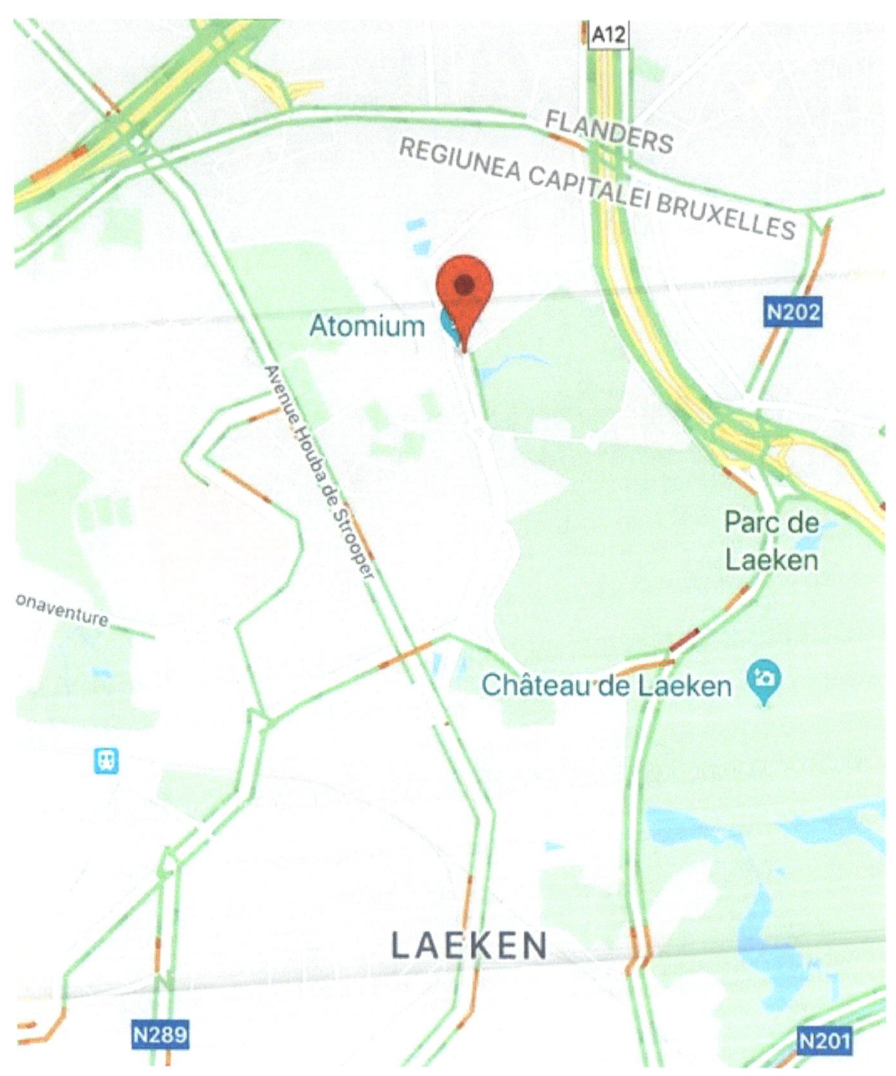

For ticket prices and
information on the visit schedule you
can access the official page
http://www.atomium.be/

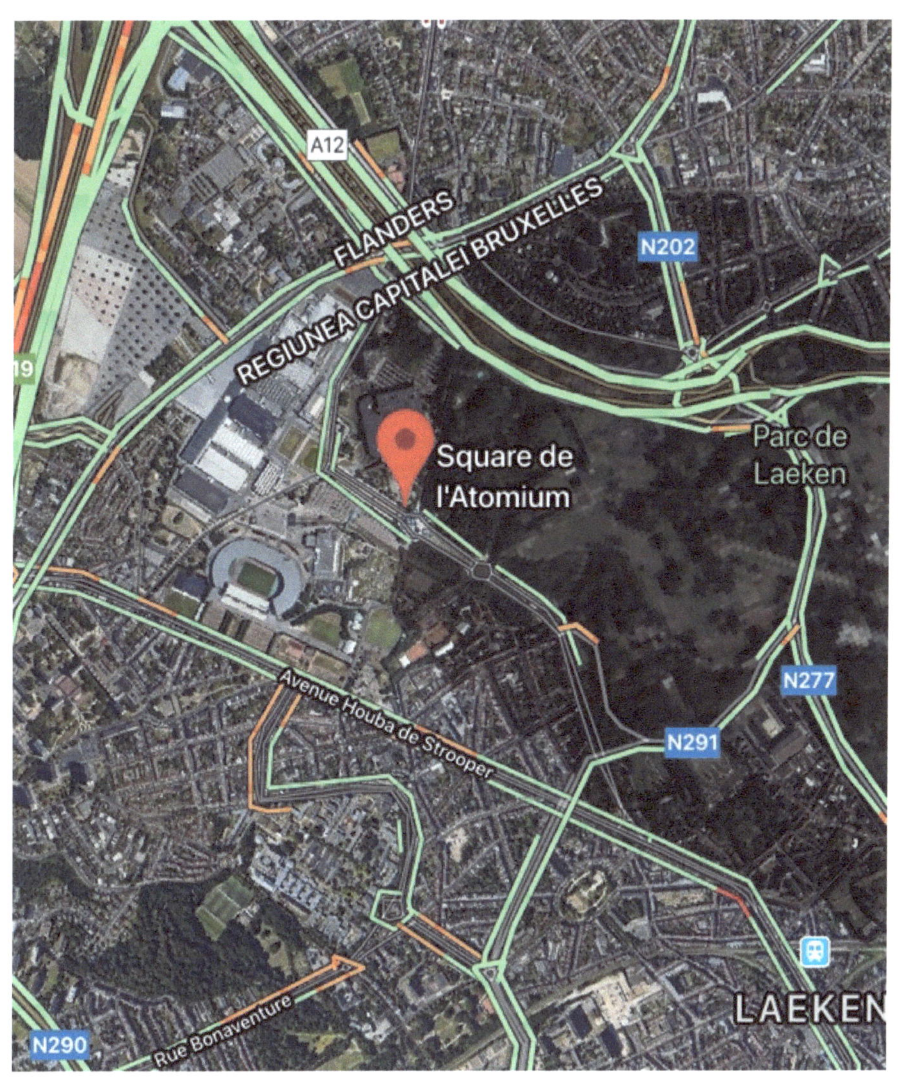